Ancient Greece
about 1000-337 B.C.

Ancient Rome
about 753 B.C.-300 A.D.

Ancient Mali
1230-1450 A.D.

Dates are sometimes noted as B.C., for BEFORE CHRIST and A.D. for ANNO DOMINI, which is Latin for YEAR OF OUR LORD, which mark the years since the birth of Jesus Christ. B.C.E. means BEFORE THE COMMON ERA and the year 1 in our modern calender marks the COMMON ERA. Since there are so many religions in the world, many historians now use B.C.E. instead of B.C., and C.E. instead of A.D, but this book uses the more traditional B.C. and A.D.

OUR WORLD
FAR & WIDE

| Columbus sails to New World. 1492 | Ponce de Léon lands in Florida. 1513 | Cartier claims land in Canada for France. 1534 | Christopher Newport comes to Virginia. 1607 | Thomas Jefferson writes Declaration of Independence. 1776 | George Washington is elected President. 1789 | Abraham Lincoln gives Gettysburg Address. 1863 | Rosa Parks arrested starting Civil Rights movement. 1955 | Martin Luther King leads March on Washington. 1963 | Thurgood Marshall joins Supreme Court. 1967 |

FIVE PONDS PRESS

OUR WORLD
FAR & WIDE

by Joy Masoff

ADVISORY BOARD

Dr. Melissa Matusevich: Professor of Curriculum and Instruction at East Carolina University and former supervisor of Social Studies and Library Media, Montgomery County, Virginia, Public Schools.

Dr. Donald Zeigler: Professor of Geography and Political Science, Old Dominion University, Norfolk, Virginia.

REVIEWERS

Five Ponds Press wishes to acknowledge the contributions and encouragement of many Virginia public school educators. Special thanks to:
Lara Samuels of Hanover County
Kathy Morrison of Hanover County
Anita Parker of Virginia Beach
Nancy Maxwell of Fairfax County
and
Dr. Virginia Yans-McGloughlin of Rutgers University
Jason Deryck-Mahlke of John Jay High School, NY

UNIT ONE: HISTORY

Copyright ©2005 by Joy Masoff. All rights reserved.
Published by Five Ponds Press, Waccabuc, NY 10597.
Library of Congress Cataloging-in-Publication data available.
First printing January 2005.
ISBN 0-9727156-8-1
Printed in the USA

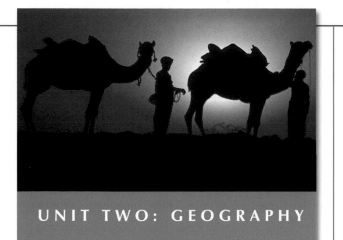

UNIT TWO: GEOGRAPHY

UNIT THREE: ECONOMICS

UNIT FOUR: CIVICS

CHAPTER 1

OUR WORLD LONG AGO

The ancient Greeks and Romans were two groups of people who made significant contributions to society in terms of architecture, government, and sports.

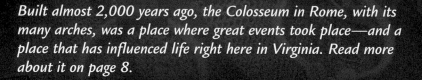

Built almost 2,000 years ago, the Colosseum in Rome, with its many arches, was a place where great events took place—and a place that has influenced life right here in Virginia. Read more about it on page 8.

The ancient Greeks were master builders. They used columns, like the one below, to build their great temples, many of which still stand today.

It is hard to believe that something that happened thousands of years ago can still have an impact on our lives today, but two mighty civilizations— **ancient Greece** and **ancient Rome**—have left big marks on the way we live.

We live in a land of freedom because of ideas of the ancient Greeks and Romans. We have built strong bridges and buildings using designs that they created more than a thousand years ago. We even meet for the Olympics every four years to celebrate strength, speed, and good sportsmanship—all because of gifts from ancient Greece and Rome.

Today Rome is a big city in Italy, but 2,000 years ago Rome was an empire—a place that ruled over many countries. It stretched into Asia and Africa. Today Greece is still a country, but it is smaller than it was long ago.

Let us travel back in time and learn more about these great civilizations…

Greek artists made beautiful sculptures. They could carve stone to look like clothing!

This map shows modern-day Greece and Italy, along with other countries on the Mediterranean Sea.

FRANCE
ITALY
Rome
SPAIN
GREECE
TURKEY
Athens
MEDITERRANEAN SEA
MOROCCO
ALGERIA
TUNISIA
LIBYA
EGYPT

ANCIENT GREECE

- *The ancient Greeks have influenced the lives of people today.*

Ancient Greece

Athens

MEDITERRANEAN SEA

Words To Know

- **Column**
  (COL-um)
  A tall cylinder-shaped pillar used to support a structure.

- **Peninsula**
  (pen-INS-u-la)
  A piece of land that is surrounded by water on three sides.

At sunset the Parthenon and its many columns appear pink and gold. It is a beautiful sight to see.

The land of Greece spreads across a group of islands and **peninsulas** that were formed when huge volcanoes exploded many thousands of years ago. These islands are very rocky, but the ancient Greeks put those rocks to good use by cutting them into blocks and **columns.** They then began to build some of the most amazing buildings in the world.

Greek Building Blocks

As Greek civilization grew stronger, it began to build huge temples to honor its many gods. Architects used long rows of thick columns to hold up big roofs. The Greeks decorated their buildings with beautiful carvings and fancy trim.

The **Parthenon** (PAR-the-non) is one of the most famous buildings on Earth. Built more than 2,400 years ago, it was a temple to honor Athena, the goddess of wisdom. It sits on the very highest point in Athens, Greece, at a place called the *Acropolis*, which means "high city."

The Parthenon has been copied many times all over the world. In fact, many of America's buildings have been inspired by Greek styles. The building in the picture above is where America's Supreme Court meets. Our penny shows the Lincoln Memorial, which also has lots of columns. Both buildings are in Washington, D.C., where there are also many other buildings designed in the Greek style.

Power to the People

Not only did we learn from the Greek way of building, we borrowed an important part of the way they lived. 2,500 years ago, the city-state of Athens was a very exciting place to live. A great "experiment" happened there. It was called a **direct democracy,** and it would change the course of history. Read all about it on page 10.

The Olympics

Are you an athlete? That word comes from the Greek word athlos, which means "contest." The ancient Greeks gave us one of the best contests in the world—the Olympics.

It all began in 776 B.C., when a group of swift runners came to a place called Olympia as part of a religious celebration.

Over time, the number of events grew from one foot race to include all sorts of sports. Today's winners get gold, silver, or bronze medals, but back then winners got a crown made from an olive tree branch. For the games, the Greeks built giant stadiums that held 45,000 people.

In 1896 the first modern Olympics were held in this marble stadium, built on the site of an ancient one in Athens. Winners got a silver medal and a crown of olive branches.

The Colosseum

At the grand opening of the Colosseum in the year 80, more than 50,000 people packed its seats. Gladiators fought, comedians performed, and men wrestled with beasts! In time, a huge canvas that covered the top to keep out the sun and rain was built. The Romans even held pretend naval battles by flooding the center of the arena.

Roman artists made many images of gladiators—from **paintings** and **scuptures**, to **mosaics** (mow-say-iks) like the one below. Notice the thousands of tiny tile pieces.

ANCIENT
ROME

• *The ancient Romans influence the lives of people today.*

"All roads lead to Rome." That was what people said at the height of the mighty Roman Empire. Some of those amazing roads led to lands as far away as Egypt. Rome was not just a city in Italy in those days. It was a vast empire that stretched from Europe into Africa and Asia.

Roman roads were masterpieces. They were good for driving chariots and wagons on and wide enough to move thousands of soldiers quickly. Those quick-stepping soldiers were the key to Rome's power. The Roman Army conquered many countries.

The ancient Romans built huge structures everywhere they went. Their **Colosseum** was as big as our modern-day sports stadiums. Whenever a new land was conquered, a stadium was one of the first things the soldiers built!

Building an Empire

One of Rome's greatest contributions to modern-day life is the **arch**. The Romans did not invent it, but they made the arch stronger and better and used it to build amazing bridges, monuments, and buildings.

By the year 200 A.D., more than a million people lived in Rome, and they needed water. Roman architects and engineers used arches to build huge **aqueducts** (AH-kwi-dukts), which used gravity to bring water down from the mountains across broad valleys to the cities. Some are still in use today!

The Romans were master builders. They also were masters at government. Our nation's founders borrowed some Roman ideas when they were deciding how America should be run. Read all about them on the next page.

Words To Know

- **Arch**
  (artch)
  A curved stone construction that spans an opening and supports weight above it.

The Key Bridge crosses the Potomac River from Washington, D.C. to Virginia using arches.

This ancient Roman aqueduct was built almost 2,000 years ago by Roman soldiers. The man in this photo is dressed like a Roman soldier in full armor. In what ways would the armor protect him?

Words To Know

- **Direct democracy**
A government in which people vote to make their own rules and laws.

This is a 2,000 year-old sculpture of Pericles, the man who led Athens to a true democracy.

GREAT IDEAS FROM
LONG AGO

- *Our government is based on ideas developed in ancient Greece and Rome.*

The Greek Gift: Democracy

When America broke away from England in 1776, it stopped being ruled by a monarch—a king or queen who inherits his or her power, or a ruler who takes it by force. America's founders decided to try something new by borrowing something old.

One of the places they looked to was ancient Greece, the birthplace of **democracy** *(dem-AH-kra-see)*. Democracy comes from the Greek word *demokratia*, which means "rule of the people."

In ancient Athens, the most powerful of the Greek city-states, people voted to make all their own rules and laws. That system, **direct democracy**, was not perfect. Only men who owned property could vote. Women, slaves, and folks who had moved to Greece from other lands could not.

Every Citizen Had a Say

Every two weeks in ancient Greece, all the men who were allowed to vote gathered at the Acropolis to discuss ideas. They then decided "yes" or "no" as to which ideas would become laws. America's founders liked the idea of government "by the people, for the people." They also wanted a land where the people ruled.

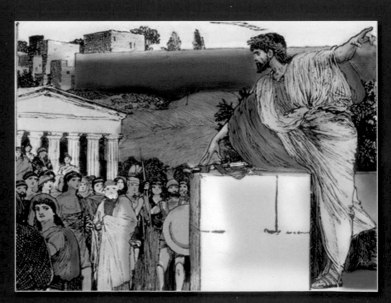

The Roman Gift: the Republic

America's founders also received a **legacy** from ancient Rome. For about 500 years, the Romans had a **republic**. That word comes from the Latin *res publica*, which means "public affairs." A republic is sometimes called a **representative** *(rep-ree-SENT-a-tiv)* **democracy** because the Romans *chose* people to represent them—people who would make the rules and laws for everyone.

Who Is in Charge?

In a monarchy *(MAHN-ark-key)*, a king or emperor makes the rules. In a democracy, no one person has all the power. People are chosen for a fixed period of time. For example, our President serves for four years. In the Roman Republic, the *consul* (president) had the job for one year and shared it with another consul!

We borrowed another idea. The Romans had three groups working together to run the country: a group to make laws, people to carry out the laws, and a group to punish law-breakers. No one group had all the power.

America also borrowed from others. The idea of "united" states came from a group of American Indians. Our legal system came from England. *All* these great ideas were stirred together to make something new.

Words To Know

- **Representative democracy**
  A government in which people vote for (elect) a smaller group of citizens to represent them and to make rules and laws for everyone.

- **legacy**
  (leg-uh-see)
  A kind of gift handed down from one generation to another.

Augustus was one of Rome's greatest leaders.

Two Classes of Citizens.

Back in ancient Rome there were two groups who got to run the country—plebeians *(pluh-BEE-uns)* and patricians *(puh-TRISH-uns)*. Women, slaves, very poor people, and foreigners had no say in what went on.

You could become a plebeian if you made a lot of money. You could only become a patrician by being born into a noble family.

The two groups did not get along with each other.

ANCIENT
MALI

• *Early Mali was a rich and powerful empire in Africa.*

• *Some of what we know about Mali's history comes from oral accounts that were handed down from Mali's storytellers.*

Words To Know

• **Griot**
(GREE-oh)
A storyteller and singer who tells all about the past.

• **Caravan**
(CARE-uh-van)
A long line of camels traveling together, carrying people and goods.

This 700-year-old sculpture shows a Malian soldier. Archers and horsemen were some of the most respected members of the community.

CHAPTER 2

Land of Gold and Glory

Africa is a beautiful continent with many different countries. Each is as different as China is from Egypt with different languages, cultures, and climates. It was here, about 800 years ago, that one of the world's great empires, the Kingdom of Mali, reached the peak of its glory.

Ancient Mali lay in an area of fertile grasslands. Today some parts of Mali are very dry, but back then there was fine soil to grow crops. There were lands for cattle to graze, gold mines to the west and south, and life-giving salt mines to the north.

The Niger River is one of the world's great waterways, stretching more than 2,500 miles—the distance from Virginia to California. The Niger cuts through the lands of Mali, and rich cities grew along its banks.

Ancient Mali / AFRICA

The Great Mosque in the city of Djenne is built in the traditional Malian way. It is made of mud! Dried mud is very strong. Parts of this building have been standing for 500 years.

Crossroads of the World

Camel caravans crossed the desert to trade for Mali's gold and salt.

Imagine a place where most people live happily. No one goes hungry. People treat one another with kindness. It is safe to walk on the streets late at night. There is music in the air and storytellers to listen to. This is what it was like in a place the people of Mali called the "Bright Country."

Because it was so safe, long camel caravans brought all sorts of wares to the great markets. They knew that they would not be robbed along the way and that folks would be honest, but one of the biggest reasons Mali grew rich was because of something we take for granted—salt! Buying and selling salt and gold made Mali the crossroads of the world.

Griots: Keepers of the Past

Many parts of Africa have a long tradition of storytellers called **griots**. They carried the entire history of their countries in their heads.

These people were the trusted advisors of kings and queens, helping them make decisions about how to rule their lands. They were very powerful people.

Today **griots** are still very important people in Africa, and they still tell stories about Mali's great kings. You will hear about those kings on the next page.

GOLDEN KINGDOM

- *Mali was ruled by rich and powerful kings.*

- *Early Mali was a wealthy trading empire before Columbus sailed to America.*

Words To Know

- **Mansa Musa**
  (MAHN-suh MOO-suh)
  A famous West African king.

This modern-day Malian salt seller sits next to slabs of salt that have been cut from deep beneath the ground at a salt mine.

Salt and Gold

Today you can find salt in every supermarket, but it was not always like that. Back in the days before refrigerators, salt was life. In fact, in some ways it was almost more valuable than gold.

Salt kept food from spoiling. It was used to tan leather and to make medicines. In the heat of the West African sun, where people sweat a lot, salt kept the body from losing too much water. Mali controlled great salt mines along with gold fields — two things everyone wanted. Salt meant life. Gold meant power!

Sundiata—The Lion King...

Sundiata (*Sun-dee-ah-tuh*) was Mali's first great leader, much like our George Washington. In the year 1230, he helped to free his people from an evil king and brought his country great peace.

The griots tell many legends about Sundiata. They say he was the son of the lion and the buffalo. He was the person who inspired the tale of the Lion King.

City of Learning

Long caravans kept arriving in Mali every day. They brought silks, gems, and spices from Asia and left with gold and salt. By the time Mansa Musa (see below) began his rule in 1307, Mali was a *very* rich empire.

Mansa Musa decided to build a great city near the Niger River in a place called Timbuktu. At the time, it became one of the richest cities in the world—and a place devoted to learning. Mansa Musa built two great universities, along with more than 170 schools. Timbuktu had a great library filled with wonderful books. People came from all over to study there.

End of an Empire

After Mansa Musa died, the new kings of Mali were not as wise. Another nation—the Songhay—attacked, and it became dangerous to travel in Mali. In time traders began to travel by sea instead of by caravans through the desert. The schools emptied, and the streets grew unsafe. A mighty empire slowly faded away.

This 400-year-old drawing shows many of ancient Timbuktu's schools and mosques. A mosque is a Muslim place of prayer. Muslims belong to a religion known as Islam. Mali's kings were Muslims.

Mansa Musa—King of Africa...

Mansa Musa's throne and ball of gold.

Mansa Musa was Sundiata's half-brother's grandson. When he took the throne, about fifty years after Sundiata died, he helped Mali grow even richer.

Mansa Musa went on a famous trip—a religious pilgrimage through Egypt to Mecca. He gave away so much gold to poor people along the way that the value of gold dropped!

THE AGE OF
EXPLORATION

• *The explorers had different reasons for going to sea, had different people paying for their trips, and ended up in different places.*

These days you can travel from one side of the world to the other in less than a day, but it has not always been like that. For thousands of years, the villages where people were born were the places where they also died, but there *were* things that made people look for new parts of the world. Hunger was one of them. Greed was another. Sometimes people were simply curious about what was "out there." Those folks all became **explorers**.

This is an exact replica of the Santa Maria, Columbus' biggest ship. It is only 98 feet long and very different from the big ships that are now built in Virginia.

Ancient Explorers

As far back as ancient Egypt, people were visiting unknown lands, usually with the idea of taking them over. The ancient Chinese were great explorers too, but the **Europeans**, starting with the Greeks and Romans, had the greatest need to push beyond their boundaries. Their early explorers went east and met people from other lands who had things that they did not have—things like gold, silver, and silks. Asia had something the **Europeans** *really* wanted—spices. Spices grew in the Indies, which is a part of Asia, and helped preserve food in the days before refrigerators.

Danger Ahead!

For many years traders brought the riches of Asia to Europe, but when the Roman Empire fell apart between 400-500 A.D, the trade routes became unsafe because Rome's once-powerful army lost control. It was difficult to travel *east* to get spices, so a few bold folks decided to try sailing across the great ocean to the *west*. Europe's first explorers did not know how big that mysterious ocean was or if they would find a huge continent. That did not stop them.

"Where Am I and Who Are You?"

The explorers made a lot of mistakes! They hoped the ocean was small, but their trips took months. When they finally reached land, they thought they were in the Indies, so they called the people living there Indians. When they realized they had landed on a continent, they tried to find a passage—perhaps a river—that cut across it and led to Asia.

Exploring was dangerous work. Hundreds of explorers dreamed of becoming rich finding new lands. Many died trying.

Words To Know

- **Explorer**
  (ex-PLORE-ur)
  A person who travels seeking new discoveries.

- **European**
  (Your-a-PEA-in)
  A person from one of the countries in Europe.

The Vikings, who lived in Northern Europe, made it as far as Canada 400 years before Columbus made his famous trip. They set up a small colony called Vinland. A colony is formed when a group of people leave their country to go live in a new land. The Vikings left Vinland and went home after many fights with the natives.

Vikings' route

Columbus' route

EUROPE

NORTH AMERICA

Bahamas

The Atlantic Ocean

AFRICA

SOUTH AMERICA

17

CHRISTOPHER COLUMBUS

• *First European to discover a direct sea route to America.*

• *Explored the "New World" beginning with his landing on an island in the Bahamas that he named San Salvador.*

Columbus made four voyages to the New World. Match the color with the lines on the map to see where he went each time.

| 1st voyage |
| 2nd voyage |
| 3rd voyage |
| 4th voyage |

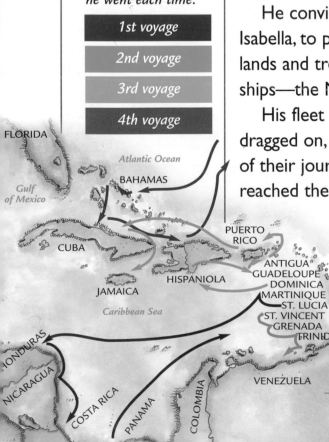

West, Not East

On the morning of August 3, 1492, Christopher Columbus, an Italian-born sailor, set off to do something no one had done before. Like most educated people of his day, he knew the world was round. He hoped that a person could reach Asia by sailing west across the great sea that rimmed Europe. The only thing he did not know was how big that ocean was.

He convinced the King and Queen of Spain, Ferdinand and Isabella, to pay for his trip by promising to give Spain any lands and treasures he found. In return, they gave him three ships—the Niña, the Pinta, and the Santa Maria.

His fleet could only cover about 150 miles a day. The trip dragged on, and his crew grew scared. Finally on the 70th day of their journey, they spotted land. Columbus thought he had reached the Indies, so he called the natives "Indians."

He did not find any gold on his first voyage, although on later trips he did. Instead, he found a "New World" for Spain to explore. Columbus was not the first person to "discover" America, but he opened a path between the Old World and the New and changed life forever for both.

JUAN
PONCE DE LÉON

- *First European to land in Florida.*
- *Claimed the land of Florida for Spain.*

"Give Me Gold!"

One of the men on Columbus' second voyage was a Spanish soldier who dreamed of getting rich—Juan Ponce de Léon. He stayed in the New World to find his fortune. In 1508 he conquered what is now Puerto Rico and became its first governor. He made a fortune in mining gold, trading slaves, and stealing land before being pushed out of office.

In April of 1513 Ponce de Léon became the first European to land on the mainland of what would one day become the United States. Legends tell us that he sailed to Florida to look for the *Fountain of Youth*—a magical spring that would give eternal life to anyone who drank from it. All he *really* wanted was more gold, more slaves, and more land to govern. He named the land he found *Pascua de Florida,* which means "feast of flowers," and claimed it for Spain. He also built a little settlement that he called St. Augustine, but he did not find gold, so Ponce de Léon kept looking.

In 1521 he returned to Florida to explore the west coast. His ship was met by natives with bows and poisoned arrows. Ponce de Léon was shot and soon died from his wounds, but he gave Europe its first settlement in what was to become the United States of America.

There have been many stories about the Fountain of Youth. An artist painted this imaginative scene of Ponce de Léon and his men landing in Florida and testing the waters.

There was no Fountain of Youth, but you can see Ponce de Léon's first fort, which still stands in St. Augustine, Florida.

St. Augustine

FLORIDA

Atlantic Ocean

Gulf of Mexico

San Salvador

YUCATAN

Caribbean Sea

CUBA

HISPANIOLA

PUERTO RICO

QUEBEC

UDSON BAY

ONTARIO

Quebec

Montreal

JACQUES
CARTIER

- *Explored the St. Lawrence River Valley and gave France a North American claim.*

- *Helped to establish French colonies in the New World.*

"I Claim This Land for France."

In 1534, 42 years after Columbus made his amazing voyage, Jacques Cartier *(ZHOCK CAR-tee-ay)*, a curious Frenchman, set off on a journey of his own. Like the other explorers, he was trying to find a western sea route to Asia, but the King of France also wanted Cartier to claim new lands for France.

Cartier left France with two ships and crossed the Atlantic in 20 days. After passing Newfoundland *(NEWF-ind-land)*, Cartier explored the mouth of the St. Lawrence River in present-day Canada. He returned a few years later, and with the help of Native American guides, he explored the St. Lawrence River and sailed past the land that would one day became Quebec and Montreal.

The French explorers saw that there were many furry animals in the New World. Animal skins were very valuable because many parts of Europe can be cold, and most homes were not well heated. Fur coats kept people warm. Beaver skins were especially prized, and the French quickly began trading with the first Americans, who were great hunters.

CHRISTOPHER NEWPORT

- *Brought the first colonists to Jamestown, Virginia, and made three more voyages to America.*

- *One of the first Europeans to explore the James River.*

Bound for Virginia

King James of England knew other countries were claiming land in the New World. He wanted to do the same. In 1605 he hired Christopher Newport to explore the North American coast.

On a frosty December day in 1606, Captain Newport set sail for America aboard the *Susan Constant,* along with two other ships. These boats carried more than 100 men and boys who hoped to start the first permanent English colony in America. They landed on a swampy peninsula in Virginia, built a fort, and called it Jamestown, in honor of their king.

Newport explored the waters around Jamestown, sailing up the river he also named after King James. He reached the river's fall line—rapids near the western edge of the coastal plain—in what is now Richmond. John Smith (who gained fame because of the Pochantas legend) was aboard Newport's ship, along with a group of "gentlemen" who were ill-suited for the harsh life in the new colony. Most did not survive, but Newport made three more trips to North America. He played a big role in Virginia's history.

This is an exact replica of the HMS Susan Constant, *the ship that Christopher Newport sailed on his first trip to Virginia.*

CHAPTER 4

DIFFERENT LANDS AND LIVES

Every land has its own special features that affect the way people live.

Characteristics

(CAHR-ick-tur-is-tix)
Details that describe a person or place such as size, shape, or the way something looks.

Virginia has rivers, bays, mountains, and valleys. Because of these things, we have developed all sorts of skills to help us live here. We build huge ships because the waters are important to us, and we grow crops that do well with our weather and soil. All these things make us a little different from other states.

Other lands also have their own special features. Those **characteristics** have a lot to do with the reasons each place develops the way it does.

Ancient Greece and Rome were located in and around the Mediterranean Sea. The empire of Mali sat in the western part of the continent of Africa. They were all *very* different, yet each became great.

The land of Greece includes many islands in the Mediterranean Sea. These islands are very hilly with dry, rocky soil. Some have mountains, but still the ancient Greeks settled on them and managed to thrive.

Physical Characteristics

What was the land like in…

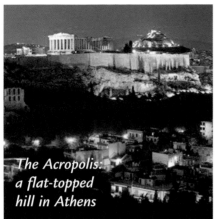

The Acropolis: a flat-topped hill in Athens

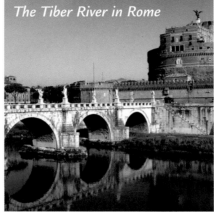

The Tiber River in Rome

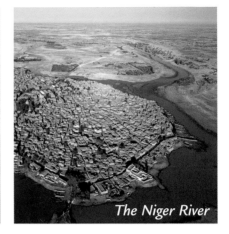

The Niger River

ANCIENT GREECE

- Surrounded by the Mediterranean Sea
- Located among mountains and hills
- Limited rich soil

ANCIENT ROME

- Located next to the Tiber River and near the Mediterranean Sea
- Built on many hills
- Limited rich soil

ANCIENT MALI

- Located near the Niger River in West Africa
- Both desert and land good for farming
- Gold mines

Human Characteristics

What did the people do in…

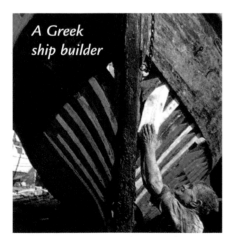

A Greek ship builder

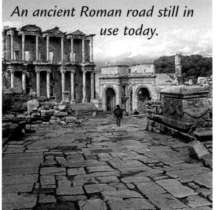

An ancient Roman road still in use today.

A modern Mali miner

ANCIENT GREECE

- Farmers
- Ship builders
- Traders

ANCIENT ROME

- Farmers
- Road builders
- Traders

ANCIENT MALI

- Farmers
- Miners
- Traders

COMPARING
EMPIRES

- *People adapt to their environment in different ways.*

Greece has rugged mountains and islands surrounded by the sea. Rome is hilly, and the soil is not rich. Mali is dry and extremely hot with areas of desert and scrubby grasslands. The three lands are very different, but they all have something in common. The people who lived there learned how to put the land to work.

Greek and Roman farmers learned to cut flat areas called "terraces" into hills so they could plant crops that thrived. In Mali, mines were dug to bring gold and salt to the people. Rivers and oceans became well-traveled "roadways." All three lands prospered and grew rich.

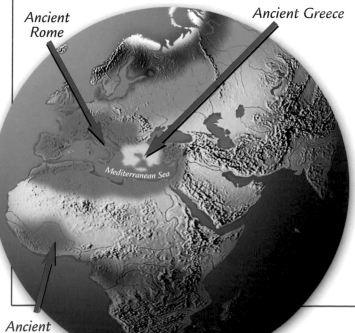

Ancient
Rome

Ancient Greece

Mediterranean Sea

Ancient
Mali

A Greek farm

Many hills and mountains made farming difficult for the ancient Greeks. They terraced the hills to farm.

A Greek island today

Greece has many islands. Greek merchants sailed the Mediterranean Sea trading with others.

Greece's rugged mountains

Many mountains led to the development of small, independent villages.

ANCIENT ROME   # ANCIENT MALI

Olive trees

The people of ancient Rome also terraced their hillsides to farm.

Caravans still cross the desert even today.

Mali has a hot climate, and people sweat a lot. Salt, a valuable natural resource, helps keep them alive.

On a Roman ship if there was no wind, men had to row.

Like the Greeks, the Romans built ships. They sailed the Mediterranean and traded with other lands.

A modern marketplace in front of a great mosque in Mali.

In ancient times, slabs of salt were traded for gold in markets like this one.

Aquaducts moved water from one place to another.

The Romans used their resources to expand their civilization to far-away places.

Parts of this mosque in Mali are hundreds of years old.

There was very little stone or wood in Mali, so people built with mud. The results were amazingly beautiful.

CHAPTER 5

MASTERING
THE GLOBE

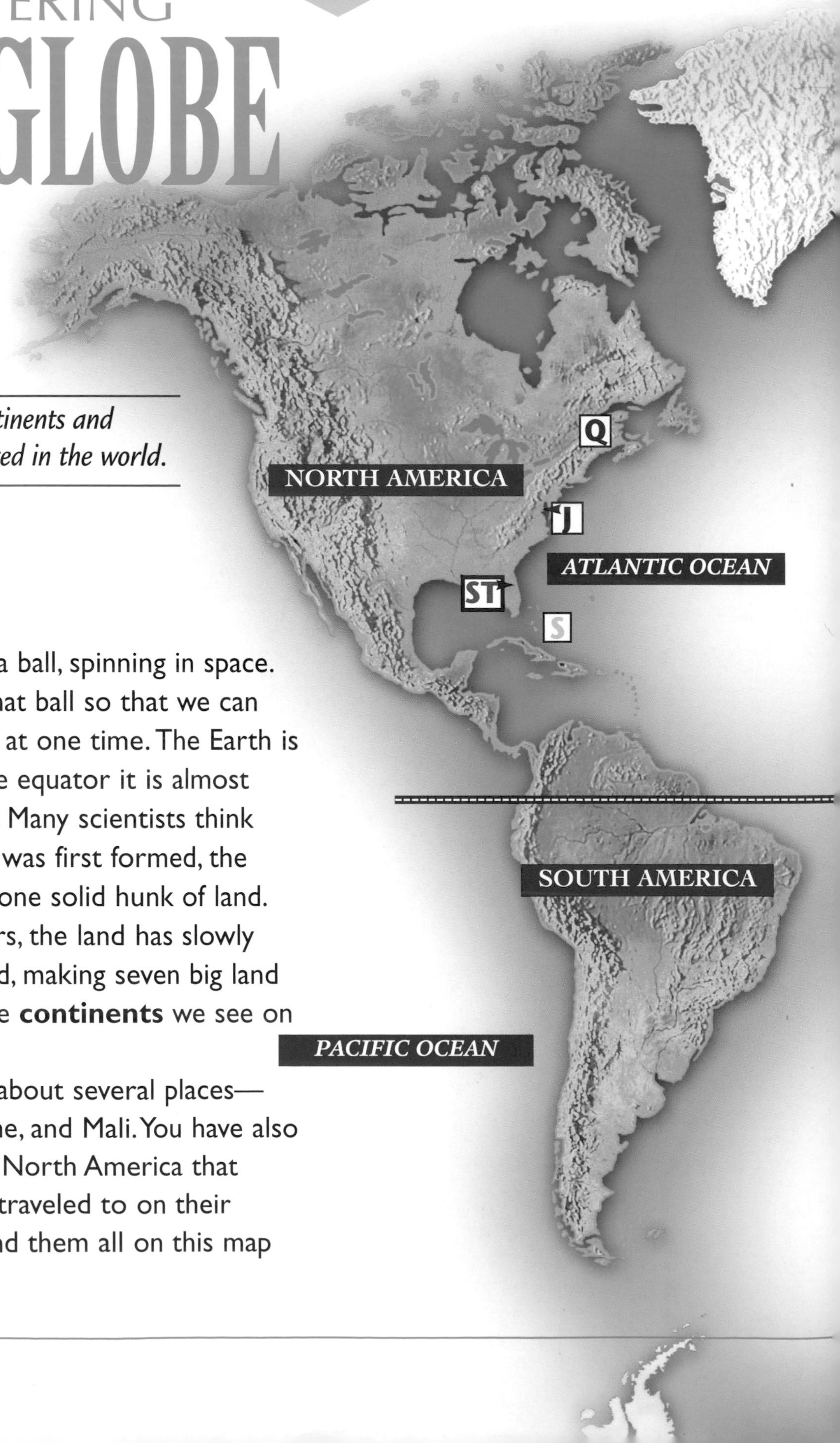

• *There are seven continents and four major oceans located in the world.*

NORTH AMERICA

Q

J

ATLANTIC OCEAN

ST

S

Our Earth is like a ball, spinning in space. Mapmakers flatten that ball so that we can see the entire world at one time. The Earth is a huge sphere. At the equator it is almost 25,000 miles around. Many scientists think that when the Earth was first formed, the continents made up one solid hunk of land. Over millions of years, the land has slowly split apart and drifted, making seven big land masses. These are the **continents** we see on the map today.

You have learned about several places—ancient Greece, Rome, and Mali. You have also read about places in North America that European explorers traveled to on their journeys. Can you find them all on this map of the world?

SOUTH AMERICA

PACIFIC OCEAN

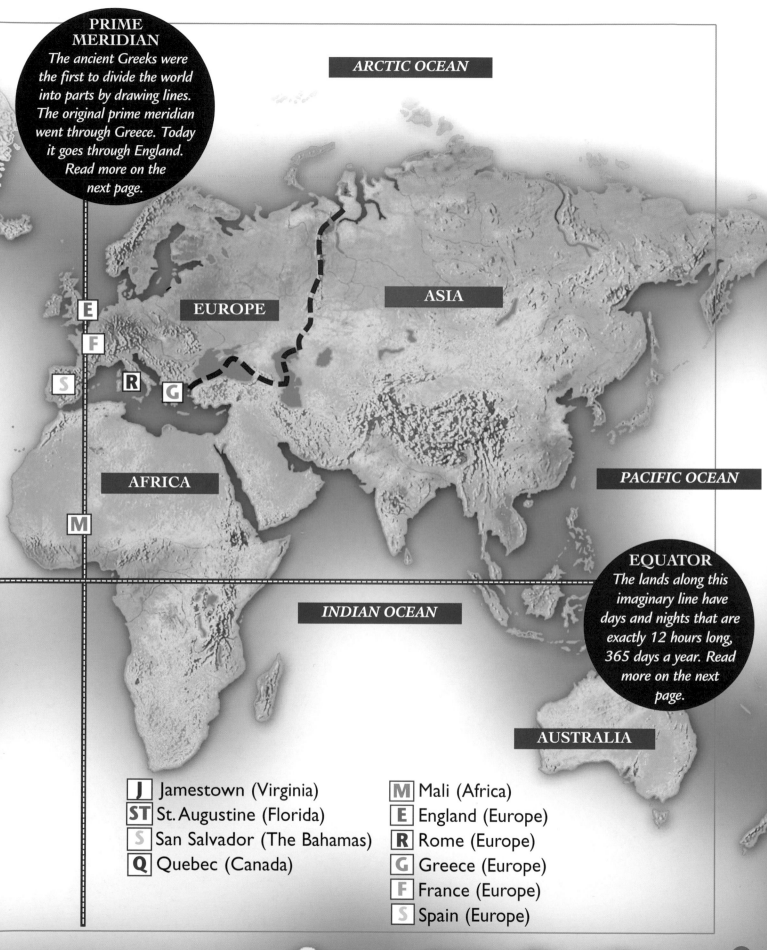

PRIME MERIDIAN
The ancient Greeks were the first to divide the world into parts by drawing lines. The original prime meridian went through Greece. Today it goes through England. Read more on the next page.

ARCTIC OCEAN

ASIA

EUROPE

E

F

S

R

G

AFRICA

M

PACIFIC OCEAN

EQUATOR
The lands along this imaginary line have days and nights that are exactly 12 hours long, 365 days a year. Read more on the next page.

INDIAN OCEAN

AUSTRALIA

J Jamestown (Virginia)
ST St. Augustine (Florida)
S San Salvador (The Bahamas)
Q Quebec (Canada)

M Mali (Africa)
E England (Europe)
R Rome (Europe)
G Greece (Europe)
F France (Europe)
S Spain (Europe)

ANTARCTICA

DIVIDING THE PLANET

Words To Know

- **Hemisphere**

  (HEM-iss-fear)
  Half of a sphere (globe) created by the prime meridian or the equator.

- *The equator and the prime meridian divide the globe into four hemispheres.*

- *A simple letter-number grid system on maps is used to locate places.*

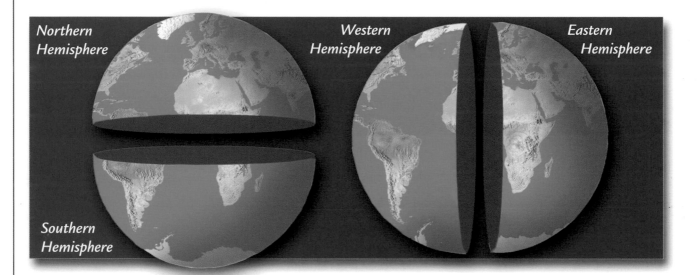

Northern Hemisphere

Southern Hemisphere

Western Hemisphere

Eastern Hemisphere

- **Prime meridian**

  An imaginary line that (when extended completely around the earth) divides the globe into the eastern and western hemispheres.

- **Equator**
  (ee-KWAY-tur)
  An imaginary line around the middle of the Earth that divides the globe into the northern and southern hemispheres.

If you took a baseball and sliced it in half, you would have a **hemisphere**. *Sphere* (*sfeer*) is another word for a round ball. *Hemi* means "half" in Latin, the language of ancient Rome.

The **equator** divides the world into the northern and southern hemispheres. When it is winter in the northern hemisphere, it is summer in the southern hemisphere.

The **prime meridian** is a make-believe line that connects the North and South Poles and passes through Greenwich, England, near London. If extended completely around the world, it divides the earth into the eastern and western hemispheres.

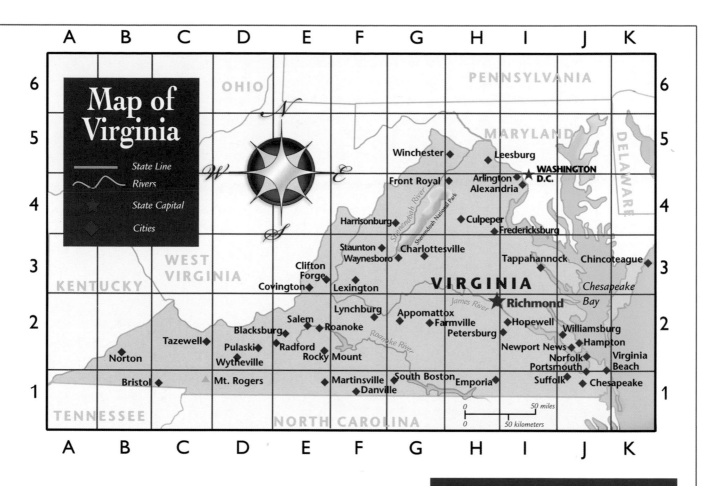

From Big to Small

Long ago, mapmakers found that it was easier if they divided maps into smaller pieces. They did this by drawing up-and-down lines and side-to-side lines to make **grids**. They labeled the grids with letters and numbers. Then they made a list of the locations of places on each map using the letter-number combinations. If you look at the map above, Tazewell is in C-2. Hampton is in J-2.

A Book of Maps

The next time you are at the library, check out an **atlas**. These map books are named after Atlas, a man who was a character in an ancient Greek myth. After he bragged about how strong he was, the gods punished him by having him carry the entire Earth on his shoulders forever!

Where Are They?

Using the grid above, see if you can answer these questions about Virginia.

1. What cities (marked by red diamonds) are in grid cell G-2?

2. What cities are in grid cell F-3?

3. What three states meet in grid cell H-5?

4. In what grid cell is Culpeper?

5. Which grid cell has the most cities?

(Answers are on page 64.)

CHAPTER 6

LOOKING AT
OUR WORLD

- *Use maps, tables, graphs, charts, and pictures to classify information.*

Maps are drawings of our planet, but we can also use other visual aids to tell stories about the world. What conclusions can you come to after studying these different pictures, charts, and graphs? Can you answer these three questions?

1. What Do These Places Have in Common?

Pictures and charts can help us classify information. This chart compares four places using geography. Which share the same characteristics? Which are most different?

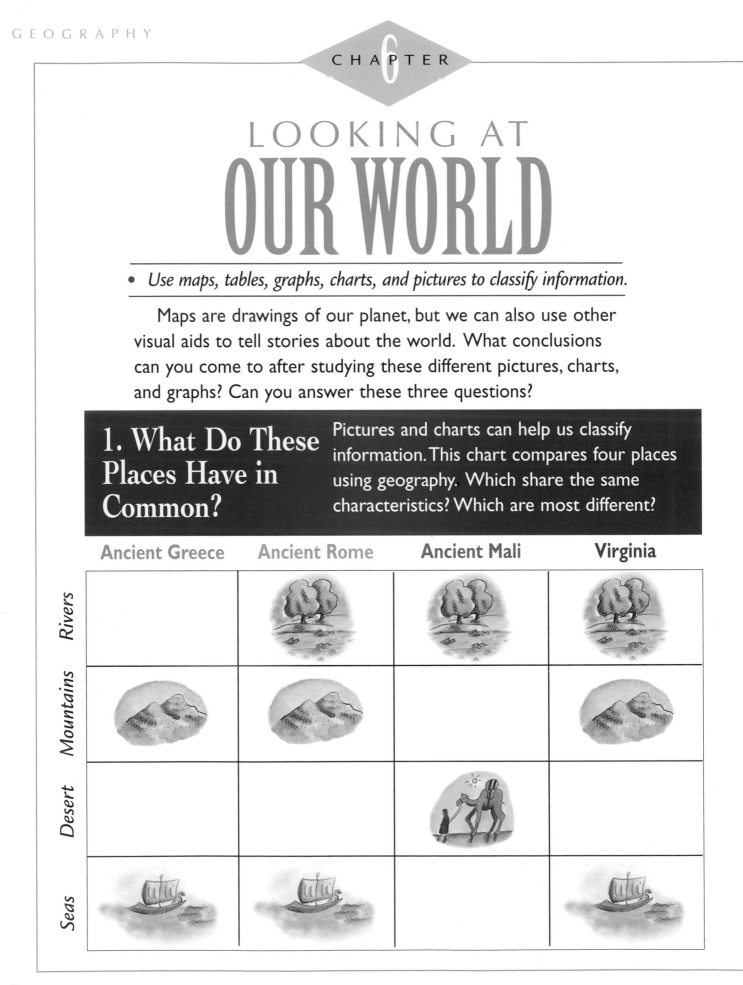

	Ancient Greece	Ancient Rome	Ancient Mali	Virginia
Rivers		🌳	🌳	🌳
Mountains	⛰	⛰		⛰
Desert			🐫	
Seas	⛵	⛵		⛵

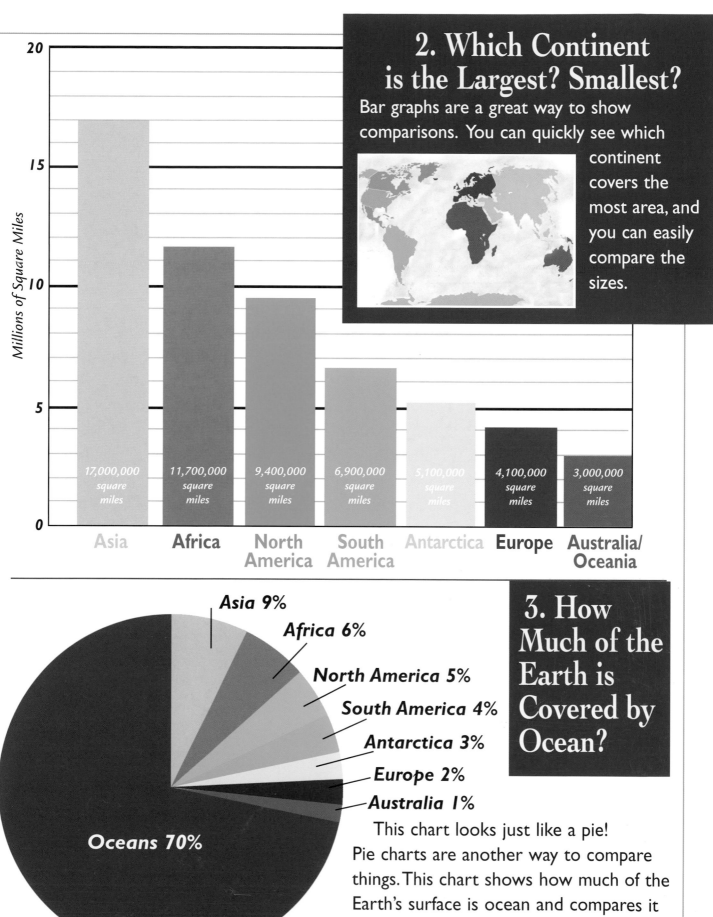

Millions of Square Miles

20

15

10

5

0

| 17,000,000 square miles | 11,700,000 square miles | 9,400,000 square miles | 6,900,000 square miles | 5,100,000 square miles | 4,100,000 square miles | 3,000,000 square miles |

Asia — Africa — North America — South America — Antarctica — Europe — Australia/Oceania

2. Which Continent is the Largest? Smallest?

Bar graphs are a great way to show comparisons. You can quickly see which continent covers the most area, and you can easily compare the sizes.

Asia 9%

Africa 6%

North America 5%

South America 4%

Antarctica 3%

Europe 2%

Australia 1%

Oceans 70%

3. How Much of the Earth is Covered by Ocean?

This chart looks just like a pie! Pie charts are another way to compare things. This chart shows how much of the Earth's surface is ocean and compares it to each of the continents.

CHAPTER 7

THE WORLD'S RESOURCES

- *Resources are used to produce (make) goods and services for consumers.*
- *Producers of goods and services need natural, human, and capital resources.*

Words To Know

- **Natural resources**
Materials that come from nature.

- **Human resources**
People working to produce goods and services.

- **Capital resources**
Goods made by people and used to produce other goods and services.

The next time you eat a bowl of cereal, think about what goes into those flakes, puffs, or pops. There are **natural resources**—the wheat the cereal is made from and the trees that were cut down to make paper for the box. There are **human resources**—farmers who grow the wheat, people who bake the flakes, the designers who create the box art, and the cashier who rings up your purchase. There are **capital resources**—machines that cut the wheat, factories where the flakes are made, trucks that bring the boxes of cereal to grocery stores, and so much more. Everything is connected!

Natural resources (sand to make concrete), human resources (drivers and engineers), and capital resources (machines) are all busy working together.

Important Natural Resources

WOOD
- Used to build houses, produce paper, make cardboard boxes, and more!

COAL
- Used to make steel, produce electricity, make plastics, and more!

WATER AND SOIL
- Both needed to grow crops. Water is also used to make electricity, and more!

Human Resources

PEOPLE MAKING THINGS
- Factory workers, construction workers, garment workers, artists, and more!

PEOPLE SERVING PEOPLE
- Teachers, doctors, nurses, lawyers, barbers, mechanics, musicians, waiters, police, and more!

Capital Resources

MACHINES
- Things that do work: bulldozers, computers, lawn mowers, and more!

TOOLS
- Things to help you do a job: hammers, nails, rakes, and more!

BUILDINGS
- Places to work: fire houses, stores, factories, hospitals, and more!

Specialization: People Doing What They Do Best

A model of an ancient Greek trading ship

The ancient Greeks and Romans were master ship-builders. They depended on the seas for trade. They also farmed and made pottery.

In the empire of Mali, some people specialized in growing food and raising cattle, while others worked to protect the land by becoming soldiers.

A statue of an ancient Malian archer

Interdependence: People Needing Other People

The ancient Greeks and Romans traded goods, such as grapes and olives, with people in parts of Asia and Africa.

The people of Mali traded gold with people from Europe, Asia, and Africa.

Gold is very valuable because it is rare.

CHAPTER 8

THINGS WE WANT AND NEED

• *Economic specialization and interdependence existed in the production of goods and services in the past and exist in our present-day communities.*

A bulldozer moves a mountain of mined coal.

What do the people of Virginia do well? Often geography influences what a person or company decides to **produce**.

We have a long coastline on the east. We have mountains in the west filled with coal. So, among other things, we **specialize** in building boats and mining coal.

Think about it. People in lands with no rivers, bays, or oceans are not going to be very good at building boats, but if you live in a place surrounded by water, you will *need* boats—**goods** that satisfy your wants. A **producer** will have to make those items by buying steel and all the other materials needed to build ships. Producers will also need to hire people with special skills to repair the ships, offering **services** to keep the fleet running smoothly.

I Need You, You Need Me

Often someone needs something that another person has. A car maker needs steel to build trucks and automobiles. Steel workers need cars to get to their jobs. This is called **economic interdependence**. Those are two big words for a very simple idea.

Virginia is famous for ship building. The aircraft carrier USS *Harry S. Truman* (shown below), was built in Newport News, a city with an **economic specialization** in building boats. Even though we build these huge ships, we depend on goods and services that come from other parts of the world!

Virginia has coal mines, so we sell coal to other states and countries, but we have no oil to heat our homes or gas to run our cars. We must buy oil and gas from other places. We rely on others for many of the things we need to live.

The amazing Virginia-built aircraft carrier, USS Harry S. Truman, *is longer than three football fields!*

Words To Know

- **Producers**
(Pro-DOO-sirs)

People who use resources to make goods and/or provide services.

- **Goods**

Things that people make or use to satisfy needs and wants.

- **Services**

Activities that satisfy people's needs and wants.

- **Economic specialization**
(ECK-uh-nom-ick Spesh-uh-li-ZAY-shun)

Focusing on one product or service.

- **Economic interdependence**
(ECK-uh-nom-ick In-ter-duh-PEN-dense)

Two or more people depending on each other for goods and services.

CHAPTER 9

MAKING CHOICES

Words To Know

- **Economic choice**
The choice of, or decision among, alternatives or possibilities.

- **Opportunity cost**
What is given up when a decision is made.

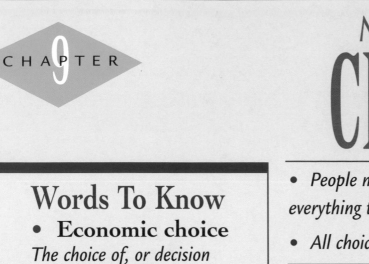

• *People make choices because they cannot have everything they want.*

• *All choices require giving something up.*

Do you get an allowance? Have you ever received a birthday card with money tucked in it? It is nice to have all that money, but it is sometimes hard to decide what to spend it on. There are so many good things to do with it!

One Big Thing?

Some items cost a lot, such as the hottest new video games. You could buy fistfuls of candy for the price of one game, but the candy will not last, while you will have the game for a long time. You might save your money for something really big, such as a new bike or a nifty skateboard. Or you could give some of your money to charity and help someone needy.

You have to make an **economic choice**. Sometimes it is not easy, since many choices require giving something else up!

This boy has made a good choice. He has decided to give some of his money to charity.

"I Can't Decide"

Imagine that you have just received $20 and have gone to a big toy store to spend it. You have to make an economic choice. You would like a new set of Legos™, but you are also tempted by a brand-new DVD of a movie you love.

You have to compare the two. If you buy the DVD, you will lose the opportunity to build cool things with the blocks—the **opportunity cost**. If you choose the blocks, you will miss the opportunity to watch that great movie. What would *you* buy?

One girl bought popcorn. The other chose ice cream. One way they can have a bit of both is if they share!

Making Economic Choices

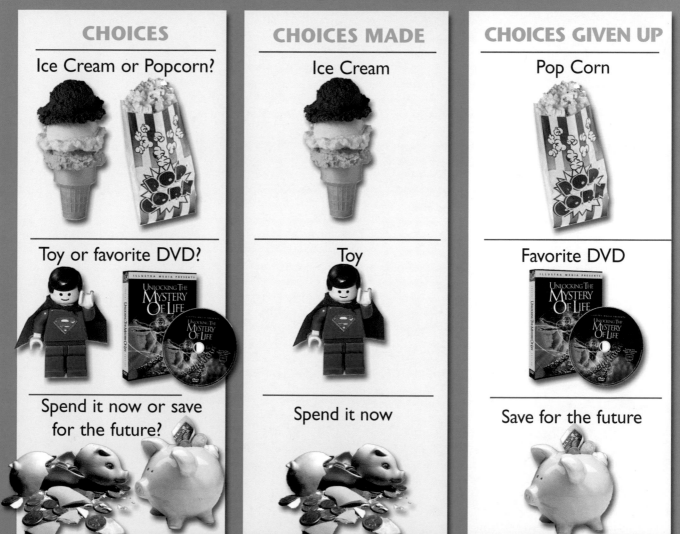

CHOICES	CHOICES MADE	CHOICES GIVEN UP
Ice Cream or Popcorn?	Ice Cream	Pop Corn
Toy or favorite DVD?	Toy	Favorite DVD
Spend it now or save for the future?	Spend it now	Save for the future

CHAPTER 10

Mount Rushmore—a huge stone monument in South Dakota—honors four of our Presidents: Washington, Jefferson, Teddy Roosevelt, and Lincoln. Read more about them on pages 42-46.

Words To Know

- **Community**
A place where people live, work, and play.

- **Rules**
What people must or must not do.

- **Laws**
Rules people live by.

- **Government**
A group of people who make rules and laws, carry out rules and laws, and decide if rules and laws have been broken.

AMERICA'S GOVERNMENT

- *Governments protect the rights and property of individuals.*

By the People, For the People

No matter where we live, be it a big city or tiny town, we try to keep our **communities** safe. We help our neighbors and lend a hand when someone needs one. We try to treat people fairly, follow the rules, and obey the laws. What exactly is a law? Who makes the laws?

Rules are things that people must or must not do. You *must* always stop at a stop sign. You *must* not steal. **Laws** are rules by which people live. They are made by our **government**— people we have chosen to make rules and laws that help keep us safe. They also carry out those laws and decide if they have been broken. If they *are* broken, our government sees to it that the people who have done bad things are punished fairly. It is a big job.

Our national government has three branches (remember those ancient Romans?) that work together. Our country's founders tried to make sure that no one branch would ever have too much power, so each branch has a say in how the others work. Here's how…

Making the Laws

Inside the U.S. Capitol Building in Washington, D.C., you will find two groups of law makers that make up the **Legislative** *(LEDGE-iss-lay-tiv)* **Branch**, or, as it is often called, **Congress**. One group is the **House of Representatives** *(rep-ree-SENT-a-tivz)*, and the other is the **Senate** *(SEN-it)*. They write our country's laws. Both groups are elected by people in their home states based on programs and ideas they present to voters.

Carrying Out the Laws

The President of the United States is the head of the **Executive** *(ex-ECK-u-tiv)* **Branch.** It is his job to approve the laws that Congress writes. If he thinks a new law is good, he signs his name at the bottom, and the law goes into effect. If he does not like it, he can refuse to sign it. That is called a **veto** *(VEE-tow)*. But the Legislative Branch can overide his choice if enough of them disagree. This way the President does not have too much power. He also gets to choose people to sit on the Supreme Court, but the Senate gets to approve each person the President has picked.

Deciding if Laws Are Broken

The folks who work in the **Judicial** *(juw-DISH-ul)* **Branch** make sure people obey the supreme laws of the land. Every state has courts, but the **U.S. Supreme Court** is the most important court in America. Once the Supreme Court makes a decision, it is final. It can only be changed by a Supreme Court decision or by changing part of the U.S. Constitution. There are nine judges on the Supreme Court. They have their jobs for life.

Our Government: Three Branches Three Buildings

The U.S. Capitol Building is home to Congress.

The White House is the home of our President.

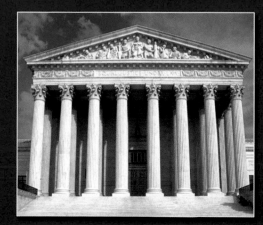

At the Supreme Court, America's top judges decide if laws are fair.

CHAPTER 11

WE, THE PEOPLE

• *Some basic principles held by American citizens include life, liberty, the pursuit of happiness, and equality under the law.*

In 1776, after a long fight with England over unfair taxes, the American colonists got fed up. America's smartest, boldest citizens got together and made a list of the reasons why the colonies should separate from England. That document was called the **Declaration of Independence**, and it promised the new Americans "life, liberty, and the pursuit of happiness."

All Men Are Created Equal

The new Americans were also promised **equality** under the law. That means that we must all have the same chances to learn, get jobs, and have a safe place to live. No one can take those rights away from us!

All this freedom sounds like a great idea, but if there were no laws at all, life might be dangerous. The new United States needed rules, so America's great thinkers got together in 1781 and tried to write a plan of government for our nation.

Life, Liberty, and Happiness: What Do They Really Mean?

LIFE means that we must all live in safety. One way our government tries to protect us from harm is by keeping armed forces ready to defend America.

LIBERTY means having the freedom to make choices—to think, feel, or choose just as you please as long as it does not hurt others.

America's first try, the **Articles of Confederation**, did not work. The States had too much power. Each did things its own way. They all had different money and different rules. Traveling from state to state was confusing, so they decided to try something new.

Freedom For All

On May 25, 1787, twelve of the thirteen states sent delegates to Philadelphia to begin work on a new plan of government—the **Constitution.** As the Constitution was being written, there were all sorts of arguments, but in the end, after a two-year struggle, the United States had a set of laws that would stand the test of time.

In 1791 the **Bill of Rights** was added, which guaranteed Americans many freedoms, including the freedom to speak openly, to choose any religion, and to print whatever we want in the press.

There were 55 delegates present at the Constitutional Convention in 1787. George Washington (shown standing at his desk) was in charge of the meetings.

Words To Know

- **Equality**
  (ee-KWALL-a-tee)
  Treating all people exactly the same way.

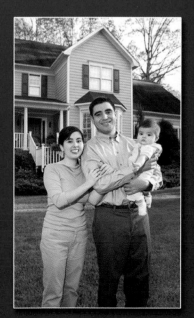

HAPPINESS comes when we know we can get decent jobs and put food on our tables. We feel happy when we have time to do the things we love. Happiness comes from having opportunities!

At times in America's past, people from other lands and cultures were treated badly. **EQUALITY UNDER THE LAW** means that we must all be treated the same way.

The first capital of the United States was in New York City. George Washington is shown riding into the city to be sworn in as President of the United States on April 30, 1789. Two years later the capital moved to Philadelphia, Pennsylvania, before finally moving to a new city built on the Potomac River—Washington, D.C.

GEORGE WASHINGTON

- *He was the first President of the United States.*
- *He worked under the new republican form of government and helped put the basic principles into practice for the new nation.*

On the day George Washington became America's first President, he was scared. He had faced death on the battlefields of the Revolutionary War, but the thought of having to be the first person to run our brand-new nation terrified him.

Even though Washington did not want to be President, he knew his country needed him. He had been given a lot of power, but he swore not to use it for his own gain. He knew that he had to be unafraid to use his power if he needed to. He also knew he needed help. The first thing he did was form a "cabinet," which is not a piece of furniture, but a group of America's brightest men, to help him.

"First in War, First in Peace...

George Washington's **FIRST** loves were his home state and his farm at Mount Vernon. He was born in Virginia in 1732 and grew up to be a fine soldier and leader.

Washington became the **FIRST** Commander-in-Chief of America's Continental Army and led it to victory over the English.

Washington was the **FIRST** to sign the Constitution and the **FIRST** to be president under its rules. He appointed the **FIRST** Cabinet (which had four members), and also chose the **FIRST** ten Justices of the Supreme Court.

No More Kings

Many people wanted Washington to be made the king of the United States. Kings are not elected. They either get the job from their parents or grab power using their armies. Kings rule for their entire lives and make all the rules by themselves. Washington believed that the President, and all those who rule our country, should be *chosen* by America's citizens. The Constitutional Convention had set up the framework for this great experiment—a **republican form of government**.

Washington took office, and slowly the three branches of the new government began to do their jobs. A national bank was started so that we all had the same kind of money. As head of the armed forces, he defended the nation against threats from others.

Washington served as President for two terms—eight years. People begged him to stay on, but he wanted to return to the life he loved as a farmer. He died two years after he left office, in 1799, at his home, Mt. Vernon, in Fairfax County, Virginia. His last words were "Tis well." America *was* well, thanks to one of our first heros.

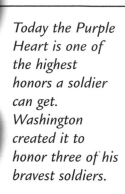

Today the Purple Heart is one of the highest honors a soldier can get. Washington created it to honor three of his bravest soldiers.

Words To Know

- **Republic**
  (ree-PUB-lick)
  A nation in which the power is given to its citizens who choose people to represent them.

First in the Hearts of His Countrymen" -Henry "Light Horse Harry" Lee

At the request of our **FIRST** President, the nation's capital was moved to a spot near Washington's home. To honor him, it was named Washington.

"We should never despair. Our situation before has been unpromising and has changed for the better, so I trust, it will again."

THOMAS JEFFERSON

- *He was born in Virginia.*
- *He was the third President of the United States.*
- *He wrote the Declaration of Independence, which states that people have certain rights.*
- *He was a leader who helped develop the country.*

It took many tries to write the Declaration. Jefferson was helped by Benjamin Franklin (at left) and John Adams (in the center)— two of America's greatest minds. Adams went on to become America's second President.

"We hold these truths to be self-evident, that all men are created equal..."

Thomas Jefferson was a tall, freckle-faced man with a secret fear. He hated speaking in public. Yet when it came to writing, he was a genius. The members of the Continental Congress, who gathered in Philadelphia in 1776, knew this. So when they needed someone to draft a document that would cut America's ties with England, they turned to the 33-year-old representative from Virgina and asked him to write it.

The Power of the Pen

The **Declaration of Independence** changed the lives of millions of people. In it Jefferson wrote that all men were created equal, regardless of birth, wealth, or rank. He said that government was the servant, not the master, of the people. These were uncommon thoughts at a time when kings ruled and people bought and sold slaves.

The 2005 nickel has Jefferson's portrait.

Who *was* the man who wrote some of the most famous words in history? Thomas Jefferson was born in Virginia in 1743. He came from a wealthy family and when his father died, he inherited more than 200 slaves. Owning slaves was common at the time. Jefferson wrote powerful words that said all men were equal, even though he kept his slaves all his life.

Freedom For All

After writing the Declaration, Jefferson returned home to make his words a reality in Virginia. He wrote the **Virginia Statute for Religious Freedom** in 1786. It later became the basis for the religion clause of the United States Constitution. Jefferson went on to do many great things, from serving as Governor of Virginia to being President of the United States from 1801-1809. During his presidency, he doubled the size of the United States with the **Lousiana Purchase**—more than 800,000 square miles of land bought from France. He also sent **Lewis and Clark** on their famous trip west to explore America.

His Proudest Moments

Jefferson's last great contribution was the founding of the **University of Virginia**. He did everything from finding the site, to designing the buildings, to planning what classes would be taught.

Thomas Jefferson—diplomat, architect, farmer, teacher, and inventor—died on July 4, 1826, exactly 50 years after his Declaration of Independence let freedom ring. We remember him as a truly great American who helped change the course of history with the stroke of his pen.

"I Wish Most To Be Remembered..."

Even though Jefferson did many great things, there were three he cared about most.

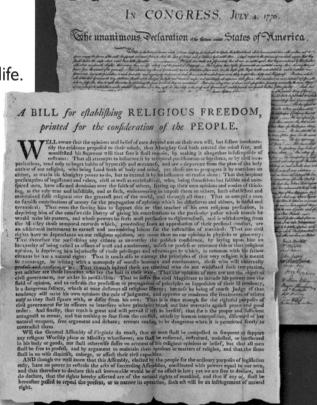

He was proudest of:
1-The Declaration of Independence.
2-The Virginia Statute for Religious Freedom.
3- The creation of the University of Virginia, which became one of the world's best universities.

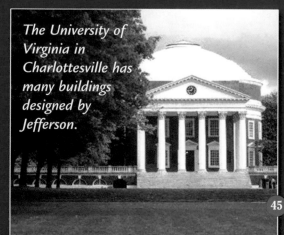

The University of Virginia in Charlottesville has many buildings designed by Jefferson.

45

From a Log Cabin to the White House

Lincoln was born in Kentucky in 1809. He came from a poor family but believed that hard work and education would help him do well in life.

Lincoln had lots of jobs. He split fence rails, worked in a store, and drove a river boat. He was a soldier, a lawyer, and a judge. He ran for office and finally became our 16th President.

Five days after the Civil War ended, John Wilkes Booth shot and killed President Lincoln as he watched a play in Washington, D.C.

ABRAHAM LINCOLN

- *He was the United States President when the country was divided over the issue of equality for all people.*

- *He helped free enslaved African Americans.*

On a chilly November day in 1863, as he prepared to give the *Gettysburg Address*, Abraham Lincoln looked sadly out at the muddy fields of Gettysburg, Pennsylvania. Just a few months earlier, the bloodiest battle of the Civil War had been fought at this very spot. More than 45,000 soldiers had been killed or wounded in this one battle. Our nation wept. Why had America been torn apart? Why were brothers fighting brothers? The fight began over slavery—the buying, selling, and owning of human beings.

The Civil War

The **War Between the States** began just days after Lincoln won the 1860 presidential elections. He had promised to stop the spread of slavery to new states. When he won the election, many Southern states, where slavery had long been a way of life, decided to start their own new country. On February 9, 1861, the **Confederate States of America** was formed. Like a family torn apart by a divorce, our nation was ripped in two.

This painting shows the horror of war on a Virginia battlefield.

Brother Against Brother

Virginia left the Union—the United States—on April 17, 1861, and became part of the eleven-state Confederacy *(con-FED-er-a-see)*. Virginia was also torn apart when its western counties chose to rejoin the Union, forming a new state—West Virginia.

Month after month the war dragged on. The farmlands of Bull Run, Antietam, and Fredricksburg became huge graveyards. On January 1, 1863, as the nation approached its third year at war, Lincoln took a bold step. He wrote a document called the **Emancipation Proclamation** and said "that all persons held as slaves" in the Confederate states (but not elsewhere) "are, and henceforward shall be free." By the war's end, almost 200,000 freed slaves had joined the Union Army.

Free at Last

The Civil War ended on April 9, 1865, when Robert E. Lee surrendered at Appomattox Courthouse in Virginia. Five days later, as Lincoln enjoyed an evening at Ford's Theater in Washington, D.C., John Wilkes Booth, an angry southerner, shot the President. Lincoln died the next day.

Today we still remember Lincoln's *Gettysburg Address*. It reminds us that we live in a land where *all* people, regardless of race, deserve the same chances for life and liberty. As Lincoln said that day at Gettysburg, "…this nation, under God, shall have a new birth of freedom—and that government of the people, by the people, for the people, shall not perish from the earth."

"As I would not be a slave, so I would not be a master. This expresses my idea of democracy."

ROSA
PARKS

- *She is an African American woman who refused to give up her seat on a public bus even though it was the law where she lived.*
- *She helped to bring about changes in laws and worked so that all people would have equal rights.*

Superheroes do not have to have big muscles or wear capes. Sometimes very ordinary people perform super-acts. Rosa Parks, a seamstress in Montgomery, Alabama, was a true superhero. She helped to change a law that no one thought could be changed, and she did it by doing one very little but very brave thing. For months she and her friends had been planning it— waiting for the right moment to make their move. That day came on December 1, 1955.

Words To Know

- **Boycott**
  (BOY-cot)
  To refuse to deal with a person, group, or nation in order to punish or show disapproval.

- **Segregation**
  (seg-re-GAE-shun)
  The act or practice of keeping people or groups apart, which leads to inequality.

"I do the very best I can to look upon life with optimism and hope ..."

A World Apart

Rosa Parks was born in 1913 in Alabama, a state with strict **segregation** laws. African Americans had to go to separate schools and play in separate parks. They had to give up their seats to white people on trains or buses. It was a time when most African Americans could not vote, and a person of color could be killed just "because."

Mrs. Parks went to college, got married, and got one of the only jobs she could—sewing. She and her husband Raymond joined the NAACP—*The National Association for the Advancement of Colored People*—a group devoted to making life better for African Americans.

The Mother of Civil Rights

On a chilly December evening, Mrs. Parks got on the bus to go home and took a seat in a section reserved for white people. When the driver told her to give up her seat to a white man, she quietly said, "No." She was arrested and put in jail!

Leaders of the black community, including a young pastor, Dr. Martin Luther King, called for a **boycott** of the bus company. That boycott lasted 382 days. The city's African Americans walked miles to work or carpooled. The bus company almost went out of business.

In November of 1956, the U.S. Supreme Court struck down the segregation laws on public transportation. Blacks and whites would now be treated the same when they rode on buses or trains, but the long struggle for civil rights was far from over. Rosa Parks would keep playing a big part in that struggle, always ready to fight for people who were treated badly simply because of the color of their skin.

One Small Step...

Until 1955 African Americans could only sit at the back of the bus. They had to give up their seats to white people.

Mrs. Parks would not get up! She was arrested, finger-printed, and sent to jail.

More than 42,000 African Americans started walking instead of riding. They stopped using the buses for more than a year until the laws were changed.

Thurgood Marshall was the grandson of former slaves. He studied hard, went to college, and became a great lawyer.

His most famous court case was called *Brown vs. the Topeka Board of Education.* Because of that victory, Ruby Bridges became the first black child to go to a white school. Grown-ups had to protect her in the beginning, and she became a national symbol.

In 1967 Marshall was chosen to be a U.S. Supreme Court judge. He was the first person of color to wear the robes of a high court justice—a very great honor.

THURGOOD
MARSHALL

- *A lawyer who defended people at a time when not all people had equal rights.*
- *He was the first African-American Justice of the United States Supreme Court.*

"Separate but equal." That was the law in the early 1900's (and before), but people were not *really* treated equally back then. White children went to whites-only schools. African American children went to schools with other children of color. Their schools were not as good as the schools the white children attended.

Unfair!

Thurgood Marshall was the man who helped change that. He was born in Baltimore, Maryland, in 1908. He was turned away from the Law School at the University of Maryland because he was not white. He *knew* he had to change America's unfair laws.

Ruby Bridges and the famous painting she inspired.

Thurgood Marshall became a lawyer for the NAACP, *the National Association for the Advancement of Colored People*. **Desegregation** and equality were his goals, and he spent his entire life working for them.

Upholding the Constitution

Marshall fought a legal battle against the U.S. military so that African Americans could become officers. His most famous legal victory was *Brown vs. Board of Education of Topeka*—the case that allowed black and white children to go to the same schools together. He believed in the Constitution with all his heart and used it to support his beliefs.

He became a judge in New York in 1961 and six years later was chosen by President Lyndon Johnson to be a U.S. Supreme Court Justice. That is the highest honor a judge can be given. For the next 24 years he worked to give *every* American citizen equal protection under the Constitution that he so cherished.

Do you recognize this building? It is the Supreme Court, where Thurgood Marshall had just won his biggest case. Little did he know he would return here to become a famous judge.

Thurgood Marshall has been honored with statues, scholarships, and even a postage stamp.

BLACK HERITAGE
USA 37
Thurgood Marshall

Words To Know
- **Desegregate**
  (dee-SEG-ra-gate)
  Mixing racial or religious groups together into a community after they have been kept apart.

"Equal means getting the same thing, at the same time and in the same place."

MARTIN LUTHER
KING, JR.

- *He was an African American minister who worked for equal rights for all people.*

- *He helped bring about changes in laws through peaceful means.*

How much would you be willing to put up with to change something you *knew* was wrong? Could you stand to be screamed at or thrown in jail? Would you give up if someone bombed your house?

Martin Luther King was arrested almost 20 times. He was beaten and got many death threats, but he never behaved in an angry way, and he never gave up fighting for the rights of his fellow human beings.

"I have a dream that my four little children will one day live in a nation where they will not be judged by the color of their skin but by the content of their character."

Martin Luther King, Jr. was born in 1929 in Georgia. His father, grandfather, and great-grandfather were all preachers. He followed in their footsteps.

At the age of 25, he became a minister in Alabama. African Americans were being treated badly in much of the South. He was arrested many times.

Dr. King formed the Southern Christian Leadership Conference in 1957 to fight segregation. One year later the U.S. Congress passed the first Civil Rights Act since the end of the Civil War.

WE SHALL OVERCOME

Between 1957 and 1968, Dr. King traveled over six million miles. He gave over 2,500 speeches. He led a huge boycott in Alabama after Rosa Parks was arrested for refusing to give her bus seat to a white man. He spoke to more than 250,000 people at a peaceful march on Washington, D.C. and dared them to dream of a land where people were judged by their hearts, not their skin. He urged people to use peaceful means to change things and taught them about **civil disobedience** as a way to make those changes. His powerful voice was heard by millions, and several unfair laws were struck down because of what he said.

The Promised Land

On the evening of April 4, 1968, Dr. King was shot in Memphis, Tennessee. Sadly, he died soon after at the age of 39.

Dr. King peacefully worked for change. He did not speak in anger. He did not hit back. His life is proof that dignity, patience, and faith can move mountains.

Words To Know

- **Civil disobedience**
  (DIS-oh-bee-dee-ens)

Refusing to obey laws that are unfair; using non-violent public protests, such as a group of people blocking the entrance to a building.

Soon after his "I Have a Dream" speech on the steps of the Lincoln Memorial in 1963, the U.S. Constitution was changed so that African Americans would no longer be unfairly kept from voting.

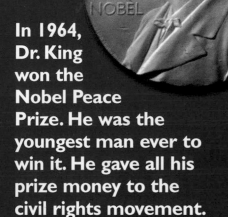

In 1964, Dr. King won the Nobel Peace Prize. He was the youngest man ever to win it. He gave all his prize money to the civil rights movement.

When Dr. King was killed in 1968, people were sad. Many got very angry, and there were riots in some cities. Today we remember Dr. King as a man of peace who died trying to make the world a better place.

Fourth of July fireworks burst over the Statue of Liberty—a symbol of freedom all over the world.

Words To Know

- **Veteran**

    (VET-ur-in)

A person who has served in the military, which includes the Army, Navy, Air Force, Marines, Coast Guard, and National Guard.

There are over 200,000 soldiers and sailors— from every war America has fought—buried at Arlington National Cemetery in Virginia.

ALL-AMERICAN
HOLIDAYS

- *America has set aside special days to honor people who have served to protect our country's freedom.*

Everyone loves a parade, and it is fun to get a day off from school on a holiday, but there is a very important reason we are celebrating. Many of our special celebrations are a reminder of people who did brave and amazing things to help make America great.

Heroes Forever

We celebrate President's Day in February to salute George Washington and Abraham Lincoln. We remember Martin Luther King, Jr. in January. On the 4th of July, we proudly cheer our nation's fight for independence.

But there are two holidays that are especially important. They do not honor famous men. Instead they celebrate the bravery and courage of ordinary people just like you.

To Protect and Defend

Memorial Day was first called *Decoration Day* because people "decorated" the graves of soldiers who had died in the Civil War. Beginning in May of 1868, family and friends started placing flowers and flags at the graves of the war's dead. Sadly, the Civil War was not America's only war. Memorial Day became a day to honor *all* the men and women who had died fighting for freedom. In 1971 Congress made Memorial Day a national holiday to be celebrated on the last Monday in May.

Every November 11 we celebrate **Veterans Day**— a day to honor *everyone* who has served in the military. November 11, 1918, was the day World War I ended. It was one of the bloodiest wars of all time. To welcome the return of peace to the world, a day was set aside to salute *all* the soldiers who had given up so much.

So this year on Memorial Day and Veterans Day, enjoy the picnics and parades, but stop and think about the people who gave their all for freedom.

Two Very Special Days to Remember

MEMORIAL DAY is always held on the last Monday in May to honor all those who died fighting for America. This girl has just placed a small flag at the Vietnam Memorial in Washington, D.C., which lists the names of all those who lost their lives in Vietnam.

VETERANS DAY falls in November and is a day of recognition and respect for all Americans who served in the military. This man is a proud veteran of World War II—one of the biggest wars ever.

CHAPTER 12

AMERICA, THE DIVERSE

- The American people come from diverse ethnic and national origins and are united as Americans by basic American principles.

In the early 1900's a great wave of people left Europe for America, hoping for a better life. They carried everything they owned in cardboard suitcases, trunks, and sacks. They were tired and scared when they arrived—not sure what life would be like in the United States.

Coming Together

Many thousands of years ago people rarely left home. They never saw people who looked different from themselves. The Africans were the first people to leave their homelands—fanning out to populate the world. Ancient Egyptians and Greeks were some of the first to write stories of what they saw on their journeys. Their explorers brought back diaries from their voyages, along with wild (and often *very* confused) descriptions of the people and things they had seen.

First Contacts

As people began to travel from continent to continent, Asians saw Africans for the first time. Europeans saw Asians.

Something interesting happened in America. It became the first place on Earth where people of so many different colors and ethnic groups lived side by side. The United States became the first place where Native Americans, Africans, Europeans, and Asians all *had* to learn to work together. America became the world's first truly diverse nation.

We would have to work very hard to make this a land where everyone was treated the same. It has not always been easy, and we have made a lot of mistakes. We are still learning.

Words To Know

- **Diversity**
  (Di-VER-sit-ee)
  The differences between people such as age, religion, and race.

- **Customs**
  (CUST-umz)
  Ways of doing things that are passed from one generation to the next.

- **Ethnic Group**
  People who share a common race, birthplace, religion, language, or culture.

In the United States, children from many different places came face to face with boys and girls who looked, spoke, and dressed differently.

These children's families come from six different continents!

WHY DIVERSITY IS
COOL!

- *Without diversity, we might not have the things that make life so much fun.*

Food: Yummy Things From Far Away

When people moved to America, they brought their favorite foods with them. Once they were here, other folks tasted these new foods and loved them!

- Enslaved Africans used ground **peanuts** in many of their dishes.
- **Pizza** is the Italian word for "pie." Flat breads with toppings were popular even in ancient Rome!
- **Donuts and cookies** came here with Dutch settlers.
- **Hamburgers** are named for the German town, Hamburg. **Hot dogs** and **pretzels** also came from Germany.
- **Chocolate** came from South America. Spanish explorers brought it back to Europe and sweetened it.
- **Tacos** and **tortillas** came from Mexico. Corn was sacred to many Native Americans.
- **Ice cream** may have been first made in China.
- **Coffee** came from Africa.

Clothing: Who Wears the Pants?

American Indians wore long deerskin leggings. The new settlers from Europe found them to be more comfortable than their own baggy breeches. In the mid-1800's a German immigrant named Levi Strauss made pants for gold miners out of denim. He used brass rivits to make the pockets extra strong. Blue jeans were born!

Music:
Red, White, and the Blues

Turn on a radio or CD player and you will be listening to diversity in action. Today's hippest tunes have grown out of the music of many lands, especially Africa. From jazz, to the blues, to gospel, to rock, to rap, to hip-hop, our most popular music grooves to an African beat.

Enslaved Africans beat out rhythms with their hands and feet because drums were not allowed. Music was a way to forget the sadness of slavery, to pray, and especially to "talk" secretly to other slaves and arrange meetings without the master knowing.

From Jazz to Rock to Rap

The enslaved Africans had "call and answer" music and melodies made up on-the-go instead of playing exact notes. That grew into jazz. Jazz is full of joy. Rock 'n' roll came along and was also inspired by the drumbeats and strummed strings of African music mixed with European melodies. Rap and hip-hop have roots that go even further back—to the *griots* of West Africa. (You read about them on page 13.)

Spicy Salsa

Salsa is a tangy dip for chips, but it is also a hot and spicy style of music and dance—a mix of African and Spanish rhythms—and it is great fun. These days music is a world-wide blend of sounds. Rappers sing to 200-year-old European melodies.
Music truly rocks!

Louis Armstrong was one of America's greatest musicians. He learned to play the horn in reform school, a type of school for kids who get in trouble with the law. He played jazz—a kind of music where the melody changed at the whim of the musician. Jazz soon was being played all over the world.

From Africa...

...to America

Break dancing and hip-hop are borrowed from African traditions, but they also mix in Asian Kung Fu moves, the Brazilian fighting art of Capoeira (ka-PWE-rah), Latin dancing styles, and much more!

Americans love to dance! Square dancing is a combination of clog dancing, reels, and polkas from Europe.

The Right to Vote

African Americans and women were not always treated as equals. The U.S. Constitution had to be changed to include them. That took years and years!

In 1867 African Americans finally became citizens of the United States. In 1870 they got the right to vote, but many were still turned away from the polls by unfair taxes or odd "rules." In 1964 a law was passed that guaranteed *all* African Americans the right to vote.

Women finally got their first chance to vote for President in 1920 after the U. S. Constitution was amended to include women.

WE ARE ALL
EQUAL

- *We are all united as Americans by basic American principles.*

You now know that Americans are united by something very special—the right to life, liberty, the pursuit of happiness, and equality under the law. These are rights than cannot be taken away.

We must all have the same chances to learn, get jobs, and have a safe place to live, no matter where we come from. We must all have a voice in the way our country is run.

Vote for Me!

You also now know that the United States is a **republic.** We choose people to be our President, governor, senator, or mayor because they have promised to do things the way we would like. In our **representative democracy** every American citizen over the age of 18 can vote for the people who make our laws. They do this by voting in elections. Every year on the first Tuesday of November, voters go to the polls—a place to vote—and select their favorite candidates and decide on important issues.

One Promise, One Dream

Our nation was born with a promise of freedom. That freedom comes from having a say in how we live. In the past we were sometimes afraid of people who moved to the United States from other lands, so we wrote laws to keep them out. Our leaders thought these newcomers might try to overthrow our government, but we have learned that people from different backgrounds can help make our nation stronger and better!

Our American Dream

Americans have always been dreamers. From the First Americans to the early settlers to our newest immigrants, we have always dreamed of a country where people of every color and every land could live peacefully. We must always remember that we are *all* Americans and we are *all* created equal. We are united by a hunger for freedom and a longing for justice and *together we* can help make America's dreams come true.

Words To Know

- **Republican form of government**

A representative democracy where we elect people to speak for us in the making of laws.

PROUD TO BE A VIRGINIA DEMOCRAT

VOTE REPUBLICAN

Today America has two main political parties— the Republicans and the Democrats. Each has different ideas about how America should be run. Every year across the country, candidates from each party run against each other in elections.

INDEX

America is not like a blanket—
one piece of unbroken cloth.

America is more like a quilt—
many patches, many pieces,
many colors, many sizes,
all woven together
by a common thread.

–Rev. Jesse Jackson

RESOURCES

Additional Reading

Ancona, George. *Bananas-From Manolo to Margie.* Houghton Mifflin School

Coles, Robert. *The Story of Ruby Bridges.* Scholastic

D'Aulaire, Ingri and Edgar. *D'Aulaires Book of Greek Myths.* Delacorte Books for Young Readers

Fritz, Jean. *Around the World in a Hundred Years: From Henry the Navigator to Magellan.* Putnam Publishing Group

Mitchell, Lori. *Different Just Like Me.* Charlesbridge Publishing

Murray, Peter. *Dreams: The Story of Martin Luther King Jr.* Child's World

Pryor, Bonnie. *The House on Maple Street.* HarperTrophy

Ringgold, Faith. *If A Bus Could Talk: the Story of Rosa Parks.* Simon & Schuster Children's Publishing

Wisniewski, David. *Sundiata : Lion King of Mali.* Clarion Books

Online Resources

http://mali.pwnet.org
   A good site for information and photos of Mali

www.marinersmuseum.org and www.mariner.org
   Excellent collection of exploration-related materials

www.monticello.org
   Visit Thomas Jefferson's home

www.whitehouse.gov
   All things Presidential

www.thekingcenter.com to hear a wonderful sound clip of Martin Luther King, Jr. and
www.stanford.edu/group/King/ which has several speechs that you can download.

Activities & Assessments

A companion binder with 48 pages of classroom activities, reproducibles, graphic organizers, assessments and answer keys is available FREE with every 25-book classroom pack. Contact Five Ponds Press at www.fivepondspress.com for further information.

PHOTO CREDITS

Every effort has been made to insure that this listing is complete and accurate and that appropriate credit has been given and permissions obtained. In the event of any ommisions or errors, the publisher will endeavor to correct said errors or ommisions in the next printing. All photos and illustrations listed below are copyrighted by the respective providers. Page 1: (TL) Digital Stock, (TM) Photodisc, (TR) Corel, (Bottom, from L to R) Metropolitan Museum of Art, Corbis, The Newport News Public Library, National Portrait Gallery, Chicago Historical Society, National Portrait Gallery, National Archives, Corbis, National Archives. Page 2: (BL) Digital Vision, (TR) Digital Vision. CHAPTER ONE, Page 3; Corbis, (TR) Photodisc. Page 4; (B) Brand X. Page 5; (TL) Digital Stock, (M) Comstock, (BR) Photodisc. Page 6; (B) Photographer's Choice. Page 7; (TL) Corel, (TR) Comstock, (BR) IOC. Page 8; (TL) Digital Stock, (ML) Corbis, (BL) Image Bank, (BM) MSA. Page 9; (ML) Photodisc, (BL) Photodisc, (BR) Corbis. Page 10; (ML) Corel, (BR) MSA. Page 11; (BL) Corbis, (MR) Corel. CHAPTER TWO, Page 12; (BL) National Museum of African Art, Smithsonian Museum, (B) Corel. Page 13 (TL) Corel, (TR) MSA. Page 14; (MR) Dan Heller, (BL) Corbis, (BR) MSA. Page 15, (BL) Bibleoteque National de France, (BR) Digital Stock, (TR) Embassy of Mali. CHAPTER THREE, Page 16; Corbis. Page 17; (MR) Corel, (BR) Digital Vision. Page 18; (B) Photodisc, (TR) Corbis. Page 17, (TR) St. Augustine Bureau of Tourism, (BR) Photodisc. Page 20; (TL) Photodisc. (BL) Photodisc, (BR) Corbis. Page 21, (TL) Newport News Public Library, (BR) Jamestown Yorktown Foundation. CHAPTER 4, Page 22; The Image Bank. Page 23; (TL) Digital Vision, (TM) Corel, (TR) Corel, (BL) Corbis, (BM) Corel. (BR) Photodisc. Page 24; (BL) Digital Vision. (TR) Corel, (MR) Photodisc, (BR) Photodisc. Page 25; (TL) Digital Stock, (ML) Corel, (BL) Photodisc, (TR) Photodisc, (MR) Corel, (BR) Dan Heller. CHAPTER 5, Page 26-27; Digital Vision. Page 28; MSA. Page 29; MSA. CHAPTER 6, Page 30; Photodisc. CHAPTER 7, Page 32; The Image Bank, Page 33; (TL) Corel, (TM) Photodisc, (TR) Comstock, (MR) Photodisc, (ML) Photodisc, (BL) Brand X, (ML) Photodisc, (BR) Digital Stock. CHAPTER 8, Page 34; (TL) Corel, (ML) National Museum of African Art, The Smithsonian Institute, (BL) Photodisc. Page 35; Northrop/Grumman Corporation . CHAPTER 9, Page 36; Brand X. Page 37; All Photodisc except for toy/DVD (MSA). CHAPTER 10, Page 38, (TL) Corel. page 39; All Corel. CHAPTER 11, Page 40; (ML)Photodisc, (BL) Brand X, (BR) Photodisc. Page 41; (TR) The United States Capitol Historical Society, (BL) Thinkstock, (BR) Photodisc. Page 42; (TL) The National Archive, (BL) Corel, (BM) The National Archive, (BR) Photodisc. Page 43, (TR) MSA, (BL) Photodisc, (BR) National Portrait Gallery. Page 44; (TR) National Portrait Gallery, (BL) Virginia Historical Society. Page 45; (BR) University of Virginia. Page 46; (TL) Corel, (ML) The National Archives, (BL) The National Archives. Page 47, Painting by Michele Anderson, (TR) The National Archives. Page 48; (TL) The National Archives. (BL) Corbis. Page 49, All from the National Archives. Page 50; (TL) University of Maryland, (ML) The Norman Rockwell Museum, (BR) The National Archives. Page 51; (BL) The National Archives. Page 51; (BL) Corbis. Page 52; (TR) Corbis, (BL) UPI, (ML) UPI. Page 53; (BR) Corbis, (BL) The Nobel Institute. Page 54; (TL) Digital Stock, (BL) Photodisc. Page 55, (BL, BR) Corbis, (TR) Image Bank. CHAPTER 12, Page 56; (B) The Image Bank, (TR) The Ellis Island Foundation. Page 57, All National Archive except BR-MSA. Page 59; (TR) The National Archive, (BR) Corbis, (BL) Photodisc. Page 60; TL, BL National Archives, MR Photodisc. Page 61; (B) Corbis, (TR) MSA. Page 63, (From Top to Bottom, L to R), Rubberball, Rubberball, Corel, Corel, Rubberball, Photodisc, Photodisc, Photodisc, Rubberball, Corel, Corel, Photodisc, Corel, Corel, Corel, Photodisc, Rubberball, Corel, Corel, Photodisc, Rubberball, Corel, Photodisc, Rubberball, Corel, Corel, Photodisc, Rubberball, Photodisc, Corel, Corel, Photodisc, Photodisc, Corel, Rubberball, Rubberball, Corel, Corel, Corel, Corel, Rubberball, Photodisc, Photodisc, Corel, Rubberball, Photodisc, Corel, Corel, Corel, Photodisc, Photodisc, Corel. FRONT COVER; (BL) National Portrait Gallery, (TR) Antique map from a private collection, (TM) Digital Vision, (BM) Corel, (BR) Dan Heller. BACK COVER; (BL) Corbis, (BM) Digital Vision, (BR) Metropolitan Museum of Art.

Answers to questions on page 29

1. Appomatox and Farmville

2. Lexington and Staunton

3. Virginia, West Virginia, and Maryland

4. H-4

5. E-2